USDA

United States
Department of
Agriculture

Forest Service

Pacific Northwest
Research Station

Research Paper
PNW-RP-571
January 2007

Growth of Bear-Damaged Trees in a Mixed Plantation of Douglas-fir and Red Alder

Richard E. Miller, Harry W. Anderson, Donald L. Reukema, and Timothy A. Max

Authors

Richard E. Miller is a retired soil scientist, **Harry W. Anderson** is a forester, and **Donald L. Reukema** is a retired silviculturist, Forestry Sciences Laboratory, 3525 93rd Avenue SW, Olympia, WA 98512-9193; **Timothy A. Max** is a statistician, Forestry Sciences Laboratory, P.O. Box 3890, Portland, OR 97208-3890.

Cover photo—Bark callousing on a Douglas-fir tree partially girdled by black bear about 15 years earlier.

Abstract

Miller, Richard E.; Anderson, Harry W.; Reukema, Donald L.; Max, Timothy A. 2007. Growth of bear-damaged trees in a mixed plantation of Douglas-fir and red alder. Res. Pap. PNW-RP-571. Portland, OR: U.S. Department of Agriculture, Forest Service, Pacific Northwest Research Station. 29 p.

Incidence and effects of tree damage by black bear (*Ursus americanus altifrontalis*) in a 50-year-old, coast Douglas-fir (*Pseudotsuga menziesii* (Mirb.) Franco var. *menziesii*) plantation are described. Bears girdled or partially girdled 35 dominant or codominant Douglas-fir trees per acre, but only in that portion of the plantation that had been interplanted at age 4 with red alder (*Alnus rubra* Bong). No red alder were damaged. Bears damaged Douglas-fir in this stand on at least four occasions between 1929 (planting) and 1991. Fully girdled Douglas-fir (six per acre in 1976) died within 2 to 14 years. Of the 29 per acre partially girdled trees, 17 percent died in the 16 years of observation, compared to 9 percent of nondamaged trees. Cross-sectional growth of surviving damaged trees exceeded that of matched, nondamaged trees by about 30 percent at three heights on the bole: 6 ft, 4.5 ft, and immediately above the damaged area. Death of six large Douglas-fir trees per acre reduced live stand volume of this species for about 6 years after bear damage until growth of the remaining trees compensated for the volume lost to mortality. Confirmation of the stimulating effects of bear damage on subsequent tree growth is needed at other locations.

Keywords: Black bear, *Ursus americanus altifrontalis*, bear damage, Douglas-fir, tree growth, tree mortality.

Summary

Black bear (*Ursus americanus altifrontalis*) damaged trees in a coast Douglas-fir (*Pseudotsuga menziesii* (Mirb.) Franco var. *menziesii*) plantation on at least four occasions between 1929 (planting) and 1991. Bears girdled or partially girdled 35 dominant and codominant Douglas-fir trees per acre in 1976, but only in that portion of the plantation that had been interplanted at age 4 with red alder (*Alnus rubra* Bong). No red alder were damaged nor were Douglas-fir trees farther than about 10 ft from the mixed stand. Bear damage in 1976 occurred in spring as commonly reported for other locations. We surmise that bear were attracted to the 50-year-old Douglas-fir in our mixed stand because these trees were more advanced phenologically in amounts of new sapwood than were trees in the pure stand. Douglas-fir in the mixed stand were visibly larger than those in the pure stand, despite greater tree and basal area stocking in the mixed stand. Completely girdled trees (six per acre) died within 2 to 14 years of damage. Tree death was delayed probably because root systems of bear-damaged and nondamaged trees were linked by grafting. Of the partially girdled trees (29 per acre) only five (17 percent) died. One tree with bark removed from 91 percent of bole circumference lived. In the 16 years after bear damage, debarked areas (0.2 to 8.7 ft^2/tree) became smaller from above the wound (0.30 ft) and from near ground level (0.28 ft), but mostly from the sides. Rate of closure (ft^2/year) was related positively to the area of bole exposed.

Average cross-sectional growth of partially damaged trees exceeded that of diameter at breast height (d.b.h.)-matched, nondamaged trees by about 30 percent at three heights on bole: 6 ft, 4.5 ft, and immediately above the damaged area. Partial girdling (40 to 50 percent of circumference) clearly enhanced diameter growth. We attempted to eliminate potential explanations for this surprising finding. Difference in initial size of damaged vs. nondamaged trees was rejected as an explanation because we matched these trees based on initial d.b.h. Also, differences in starting or ending competitive stress index (CSI) were similar for both groups. Finally, growth at breast height (b.h.) was unrelated to change in CSI. We remain perplexed.

After bear-caused loss of 11 large Douglas-fir trees per acre (totally plus partially girdled trees), live stand volume of this species was reduced for about 6 years. Stand volume in live trees recovered rapidly as growth of the remaining trees compensated for the volume of dead trees. By 66 years after planting, total stem cubic volume of Douglas-fir in the mixed stand with nitrogen-fixing alder averaged 5,626 ft^3/acre, exceeding that in the pure stand by 396 ft^3/acre or by 7.6 percent. We made no attempt to estimate losses in bole volume or value from bear damage.

Contents

Introduction

Black bear (*Ursus americanus altifrontalis*) damage boles of coast Douglas-fir (*Pseudotsuga menziesii* (Mirb.) Franco var. *menziesii*) and other tree species in western Washington and Oregon. Damage usually occurs in spring when bears remove bark to expose and eat new sapwood tissue (Radwan 1969). Kanaskie and others (1990) estimated that about 347,000 conifers (nearly all Douglas-fir) are damaged annually on 48,700 acres in northwest Oregon. More than 10 bear-damaged trees per acre is considered severe (Stewart and others 1999). Although some bear-damaged trees die, most survive. Surprisingly, however, we found no published information about the subsequent growth of bear-damaged trees. An opportunity to confirm or extend existing information arose in spring 1976, when bear damage occurred in research plots on the Wind River Experimental Forest near Carson, Washington.[1] We report our observations about mortality and diameter growth of bear-damaged trees at this location.

In an early summary, Poelker and Hartwell (1973) provided details about black bear in Washington. Based on original research and 52 responses to a questionnaire, these authors confirmed and extended results from earlier investigations (Childs and Worthington 1955). Following are their summary statements and subsequent research findings by others:

1. Douglas-fir is a preferred species; red alder (*Alnus rubra* Bong.) is not preferred, as confirmed by Hartwell (1973) and Kanaskie and others (1990). Western redcedar (*Thuja plicata* Donn ex D. Don) is also preferred in western hemlock (*Tsuga heterophylla* (Raf.) Sarg.)–redcedar forests of coastal British Columbia (Sullivan 1993). In a mixed-species plantation in southwest Washington, bear preferred western white pine (*Pinus monticola* Dougl. ex D. Don) over coast Douglas-fir of similar diameter.[2]

2. Damage is primarily to immature, smooth-barked trees; faster growing trees are preferred, as subsequently confirmed by Kanaskie and others (1990).

3. Damage is most frequent on sites of better-than-average quality and in lightly stocked stands including mechanically thinned stands. Schmidt and Gourley (1992) described black bear biology, bear damage, and some methods for reducing damage in the Pacific Northwest. They noted that bear generally prefer to peel bark from trees in rapidly growing stands,

---

[1] DeBell, Dean. 1976. Personal communication. Research forester, Olympia Forestry Sciences Laboratory, 3625 93rd Avenue SW, Olympia, WA 98512.

[2] Harrington, Constance. 2003. Personal communication. Principal research forester, Forestry Sciences Laboratory, 3625 93rd Ave. SW, Olympia, WA 98512.

yet noted that past studies found no valid explanation of why bears select some trees or some stands over others. Kimball and others (1998a) tested the preference of free-ranging bears by chemically analyzing vascular tissue of Douglas-fir foraged by bears. They concluded that bears prefer wood tissue with a strong concentration of simple sugars and a weak concentration of aromatic terpenes. After analyzing recent vascular tissue in the lower bole of Douglas-fir in nine thinning and fertilization trials, Kimball and others (1998b) concluded that both treatments increased sugar concentration and tissue mass, but concentrations of terpenes were not affected. They suggested that these results could explain the reported preference of black bears to forage in thinned or fertilized stands.

4. Some trees are repeatedly damaged during stand development, as later confirmed by Hartwell and Johnson (1988) and Kanaskie and others (1990).

5. Decay losses after bear damage are least prevalent in Douglas-fir and most prevalent in western hemlock and Sitka spruce (*Picea sitchensis* (Bong.) Carr.).

6. Complete girdling of the bole invariably kills Douglas-fir; partial girdling may reduce growth and increase decay losses. Trees with less than one-half of the bole circumference girdled often recover with little or no growth losses. Kanaskie and others (1990) confirmed that complete girdling invariably kills Douglas-fir. Effects of partial girdling on tree growth remain unsubstantiated, however.

This claim made by Poelker and Hartwell (1973: 18, 32) that trees with less than one-half of the bole circumference girdled have little or no loss in growth is apparently based on a study that simulated logging injury to boles of 60- and 100-year-old coast Douglas-fir to determine effects on diameter growth and decay development (Shea 1967). Shea removed a square of bark to expose the sapwood. The removed square was 10, 20, or 40 percent of the bole circumference at 4.5 ft. The bared, square area started about 1 ft from the ground and extended upward toward breast height (b.h.). Therefore, the larger the exposed square and the larger the subject tree, the closer the damage was to the diameter at breast height (d.b.h.) measurement point. Growth at b.h. could be decreased by damage or even enhanced either by callusing over the bared area or by additional growth caused by accumulation of photosynthate blocked by the disruption of phloem tissue above the wound.

Three or 5 years after treatment, Shea (1967) found no significant difference in d.b.h. growth. His published data follow (standard errors not published):

Percentage of bole circumference bared	Mean diameter growth	
	Stand 1 3-year	Stand 2 5-year
	- - - - - - *Inches* - - - - - -	
0	0.42	0.89
10	.30	1.04
20	.35	.94
40	.40	.82

The apparent inference (that damage had no effects on growth) is weakened because his comparisons of diameter growth of damaged and nondamaged trees did not adjust for possible differences in initial d.b.h. among treatment groups. Nor were data provided about mean d.b.h. or sample size so one could gauge the importance of this concern.

An opportunity to confirm or extend existing information arose in spring 1976, when bear damaged trees in research plots on the Wind River Experimental Forest near Carson, Washington. A preliminary survey showed that damage was restricted to dominant and codominant Douglas-fir (see footnote 1). Many of these damaged trees were debarked over one-half or more of their circumference below b.h. We opportunistically designed a study to investigate the following questions:

1. To what extent is bear damage a recurring event in this 1929 plantation?
2. At what rate do damaged trees die? When does foliage of completely girdled trees become yellow-green, then rusty red, which is detectable on colored air photos?
3. To what extent is growth in cross-sectional areas at b.h. and at heights above and below b.h. affected by increasing severity of damage?
4. Does girdling change lower bole form?
5. Is subsequent stand yield affected by bear damage?

We recognized that answers to these questions will have a narrow scope of inference, because all observations are restricted to this study area. To mitigate this shortcoming, however, we have included and contrasted basic data from others' reports.

Study Area and Methods

Study Area

The study area is located between 1,800 and 2,000 ft in elevation in the Wind River Ranger District near Carson, Washington. At the ranger station, about 670 ft lower in elevation, annual precipitation averages 100 in, with about 10 percent falling during the frost-free growing season averaging about 130 days. The unnamed soil, a moderately deep, well-drained gravelly loam derived from pyroclastic rocks, contains about 3,000 lb/acre of total nitrogen to a 3-ft depth (Tarrant and Miller 1963). This amount is about average for lands of below-average productivity in western Washington.

The plantation was established on several hundred acres after the Yacolt Fire of 1927. Two-year-old Douglas-fir from a nonlocal seed source were planted at 8- by 8-ft spacing after the 1928 growing season. Four years later, 2-year-old red alder seedlings were interplanted at 6- by 6-ft spacing to create a 90-ft-wide strip as a firebreak; this strip straddled a north-south section line through the plantation (fig. 1). These off-site alder originated from seed collected at 50-ft elevation near Olympia, Washington.

When the Douglas-fir were 48 years from seed, four 0.2-acre plots were established in the mixed stand and four adjacent plots at matching elevations in the pure stand. This original study was designed to evaluate growth of Douglas-fir in pure vs. mixed stands. These plot pairs sampled a slope gradient between a flat ridge and a small creek (fig. 1). Site index (50-year index age; King 1968) was lowest (56 ft) at the top of the slope and gradually increased toward the creek (78 ft). Dominant understory species were salal (*Gaultheria shallon* Pursh) and huckleberry (*Vaccinium* spp.).

Measurements

After bear damage in spring 1976, we inspected the eight plots for trees damaged in 1976 and earlier. For all bear-damaged trees in the plots, we recorded 1976 overbark diameter (d.o.b.) at three heights: just above the damage, at 4.5 ft, and at 6.0 ft. We measured the area of exposed sapwood by recording height above ground at the widest, lowest, and highest point of exposed sapwood (to the nearest 0.1 ft). At each of these points, we recorded total and damaged circumference of the bole (to the nearest 0.1 ft).

Where possible, we selected a nearby, nondamaged tree that matched 1976 d.b.h. and crown position of each damaged tree. We attempted to reduce differences in site quality by restricting matched trees to the same plot, yet ensured that no

Figure 1—Only Douglas-fir associated with red alder were damaged or killed by bear (note dead trees in north/south-oriented band of darker foliage (our planted mixed stand) and in east-west drainages with volunteer red alder.

nondamaged tree was a direct competitor of its damaged match. In about half the matchings, we had to select trees outside the immediate plot. These precautions helped secure statistically independent observations of damaged and nondamaged trees. We also measured these matched nondamaged trees for 1976 d.o.b. at three corresponding heights. We initially matched 23 pairs, but this number declined by 1993 to 18 surviving pairs. To increase sample size, we selected additional damaged and nondamaged trees (nonmatched), but measured these only at d.b.h.

Measurements of d.o.b. (real or assumed, where bark was missing) were repeated after the 1977, 1980, 1987, 1989, and 1991 growing seasons. This provided 1, 4, 11, 13, and 15 years of growth data on damaged and corresponding nondamaged trees. The residual area of exposed sapwood on surviving damaged trees also was remeasured periodically.

Foliage color of damaged trees was rated and coded in 1977, and periodically through 1991, as follows:

Code	Foliage color
1	Normal (green throughout crown)
2	Brown needles in interior of crown
3	Yellow-green
4	Dead (brown-red)

Change in tree competition—We assumed that growth of both damaged and nondamaged trees was influenced by size and distance of neighboring trees. We computed a competitive stress index (CSI) (Arney 1973) for each subject tree in 1974 (before damage) and periodically through 1991. This was accomplished by (1) recording the X and Y coordinates of each tree in and near the four plots in the mixed stand; (2) remeasuring or, in a small proportion, using regression analysis to estimate tree d.b.h. in specified years; (3) entering the tree location and d.b.h. data into a computer program to calculate CSI; and (4) tabulating the estimated CSI for each subject tree and year.

All live trees in the eight plots were remeasured periodically after the growing season (1977, 1980, 1983, 1985, 1992, 1995). For nonplot trees that were either nondamaged subject trees or competitors of subject trees, however, the initial (1976) and an intermediate (1985) d.b.h. were estimated from equations developed for each plot and species. Thus, the measured 1991 d.b.h. of nonplot trees was entered in these equations to estimate their d.b.h. in 1976 and 1985. Diameters and tree-to-tree distances were entered into other equations to estimate the CSI for each subject tree and year.[3]

---

[3] Computer program provided by Dr. James Arney, mensurationist, March 1994.

Stand volume—To assess the effect of bear damage on stand growth and yield, we remeasured d.b.h. of all trees in the eight original plots installed in 1974. In the pure stand, heights were remeasured on 15 trees per plot; in the mixed stand, heights were remeasured on 15 trees each of Douglas-fir and red alder. These trees were distributed across the entire d.b.h. range. All volumes for the period 1974-1995 were computed by tariff equations (Brackett 1973). Cubic volumes of all trees measured for height were computed by using the equation derived by Bruce and DeMars (1974), and tariffs were computed from these; individual tree tariffs were averaged for each plot. Total stem cubic volume including stump and tip (CVTS) and merchantable volume to a 6-in top diameter inside bark (CV6) of each tree were computed by using tree d.b.h. and mean tariff. Tree volumes were summed to give volumes per plot, which were expanded to volumes per acre.

Data Summary and Analysis

We related the survival time (years) of damaged trees to damage severity. Severity of bole damage was calculated for each damaged tree as the proportion of damaged circumference at the bole height where exposed sapwood was widest in relation to the total circumference; this is the simplest and conventional way of expressing severity of bole damage (Kanaskie and others 1990). Our analysis of survival time used an "accelerated failure-time regression model" to quantify the effect of independent variables on the distribution of survival times (Allison 1995, Hosmer and Lemeshow 1999). The method accommodates censored observations; that is, observations for which the terminal event (death) is not observed. The model determines if there is a relationship between the independent variable (percentage of bole circumference that was removed by bears) and the shape of the survival distribution, as modeled by the Weibull Distribution. The response variable was natural log (base e) of survival time.

To compare growth among damaged and nondamaged trees, we converted overbark diameters to cross-sectional area. Growth (in cross-sectional area at each of three elevations above the ground) of matched damaged and nondamaged trees were compared by separate paired t-tests.

To test whether the relation of basal area growth to starting d.b.h. differed significantly (alpha = 0.10) between damaged and nondamaged trees, we used the extra sums of squares approach in linear regression (Neter and others 1989). An indicator (dummy) variable was specified to represent the effect of bear damage and a full model was fit that included separate regression slopes and intercepts for damaged and nondamaged trees. Stepwise regression (SAS Institute Inc. 1988) was used to test whether damaged and nondamaged trees had common regression slopes or intercepts.

To compare volume yield of Douglas-fir in the pure and the mixed-species stands in 1974 and 1995 (our last year of measurement), we expressed the response variable as a difference in yield for each plot pair (mixed minus pure). We used Student's t-statistic to test the null hypothesis that the mean difference among the four plot pairs was zero. We judged significance of this and all other tests at $p <$ 0.10 by using SAS programs (SAS Institute Inc. 1988) for statistical analyses; yet we provide actual p-value so readers can make their own inferences.

Results

Incidence and Reoccurrence of Damage

Species preference—Many Douglas-fir, but no red alder were damaged by bear at this study area (table 1).

Tree size and location—Only large, 11- to 20-in d.b.h. trees (dominant and codominants) were damaged. All were located in the mixed stand or within 10 ft of it. No trees in the four pure-Douglas-fir plots showed any evidence of recent or past bear damage. Douglas-fir associated with volunteer red alder along streams were also killed by bear (fig. 1).

Recurring damage—Of the 28 bear-damaged trees found in 1976 in the four 0.2-acre plots (equivalent to 35 trees per acre, TPA), 18 percent had been damaged on one or two earlier occasions (table 1). Two of the 23 trees that survived damage in 1976 were subsequently re-damaged about 1991; one originally nondamaged subject tree was also damaged.

Severity and Consequences of Damage

Fully girdled—Of the 28 trees in the four plots (35 TPA) that were bear-damaged in spring 1976, 5 (about 20 percent) were completely girdled (fig. 2). Four of these died 2 years after girdling, the fifth tree died by year 14 (table 2).

Partially girdled—About 80 percent of damaged trees (23/28) were partially girdled by bear (9 to 98 percent of circumference was girdled). Of these partially girdled trees, 17 percent (4/23) died in the subsequent 16 years (table 2), compared to 9 percent (2/23) of nondamaged trees.

Change in foliage color—Most completely girdled trees displayed foliage color that regressed from green to chlorotic to red-brown during a 3- to 5-year period after girdling. One tree lived for at least 12 years before foliage color changed to red-brown in year 14.

Rate of mortality—Of the original 28 bear-damaged trees, 8 (29 percent) died within 1 to 12 years after removal of 26 to 100 percent of bole circumference (table 2). Based on a Chi Square test of the slope coefficients in the survival-time

Table 1—Number of trees damaged in specified years by black bear in four 0.2-acre plots in a Douglas-fir (DF)/red alder (RA) plantation near Carson, Washington

Item	Plot and species									
	1		3		5		7		Mean	
	DF	RA	DF	RA	DF	RA	DF	RA	DF	RA
	1974									
Total trees (number per acre)	220	255	235	230	220	250	355	410	258	286
Bear-damaged:										
Number per acre	0	0	5	0	5	0	10	0	5	0
Percent	0	0	2.1	0	2.3	0	2.8	0	1.9	0
	1976									
Total trees (number per acre)	215	255	235	230	220	250	355	410	256	286
Bear-damaged:										
Number per acre	30	0	40	0	30	0	40	0	35	0
Percent	14.0	0	17.0	0	13.6	0	11.3	0	13.7	0
	Combined years									
Bear-damaged:										
Number per acre	30	0	45	0	35	0	50	0	40	0
Percent	14.0	0	19.1	0	15.9	0	14.1	0	15.6	0
Re-damaged (percent)[a]	0	0	12.5	0	16.7	0	25.0	0	14.3	0

[a] $\text{Percent} = \left(\dfrac{1974 + 1976 + 1976}{1976} \right) \times 100$

Figure 2—This Douglas-fir was completely girdled by bear in spring 1976 and photographed in fall. Note horizontal pattern of tooth marks in the sapwood and also the scar from earlier bear damage.

Table 2—Severity of bear damage and subsequent tree survival at several locations

Year of damage and percentages	Percentage of bole circumference debarked					
	1-25	26-50	51-75	76-99	100	All
1976	Wind River, Washington (this report, 28 trees damaged or 35 per acre)					
Damaged trees (percent)	6 (21)	5 (18)	6 (21)	6 (21)	5 (18)	28 (100)
Died	0 (0)	1 (20)	1 (100)	2 (33)	5 (100)	9 (32)
After: 1 year	0 (0)	1 (100)	1 (100)	2 (100)	0 (0)	4 (44)
2 years	0 (0)	1 (100)	1 (100)	2 (100)	4 (80)	8 (89)
12 years	0 (0)	1 (100)	1 (100)	2 (100)	4 (80)	8 (89)
16 years	0 (0)	1 (100)	1 (100)	2 (100)	5 (100)	9 (100)
1987	Capitol Forest, Washington (693 trees, 26 damaged trees per acre)[a]					
Damaged trees (percent)	317 (46)	117 (17)	41 (6)	89 (12)	129 (19)	693 (100)
Died after 1 year	?	?	?	?	129 (100)	?
1987 (May)	Capitol Forest, Washington (302 trees per acre total in 1984)					
Damaged trees per acre (percent)	—	—	—	—	—	109 (36)
Dead per acre (percent)						
Bear damaged	—	—	—	—	—	24 (8)
Other causes	—	—	—	—	—	9 (3)
1988	Northwest Oregon (3,342 trees total)[b]					
Damaged trees (percent):						
Coastal	—	—	—	—	—	(36)
Cascade	—	—	—	—	—	(78)
Both	—	—	—	—	—	170 (51)
Dead						
Both areas	—	—	—	—	—	41 (24)
1989	Northwest Oregon (1,463 bear-damaged trees)[c]					
Damaged trees (percent)	368 (24)	298 (20.6)	170 (11.8)	128 (8.9)	496 (33)	964 (100)
Died (within 6 months):	- - - - - - - - - - - - - - - 58 (6) - - - - - - - - - - - - - - -				?	—

[a] Hartwell and Johnson (1988) terminated the study without re-inventory and assumed that all completely girdled trees would die within one year. This was not validated. Note that 48 percent of live trees debarked in 1987 (693) were partially girdled in previous years.
[b] Kanaskie and others (1990, figs. 3 and 4). Based on ground survey of trees damaged in spring 1988.

model, B = - 6.64 (2.23), p = 0.01, we inferred that the proportion of bole circumference that was debarked had a significant effect on the survival time (years until death); more severely damaged trees died sooner.

Average rate of wound closure—In the 16 years after bear damage, areas debarked in 1976 (0.2 to 8.7 ft^2/tree) gradually closed from above (0.30 ft) and from near ground level (0.28 ft), but mostly from the sides (fig. 3). Although small debarked areas calloused over within a decade after damage, average rate of closure (ft^2/year) was related positively to the area of bole exposed (fig. 4). Rate of wound closure was faster on trees with more bared wood. The linear equation for annual rate of closure (ft^2/year) was: $Y = 0.0033 + 0.0458$ damage area in ft^2, ($r^2 = 0.91$). Note that this equation slightly underestimates the true closure rate for partially girdled trees because 4 of the 23 partially girdled trees had completely calloused over earlier than 16 years after bear damage occurred. Despite more rapid rate of wound closure, debarked areas exceeding about 1 ft^2 failed to close completely in the 16 years after damage (fig. 5).

Figure 3—Typical calloused bark pattern that masks partial girdling of this Douglas-fir tree by black bear 24 years earlier.

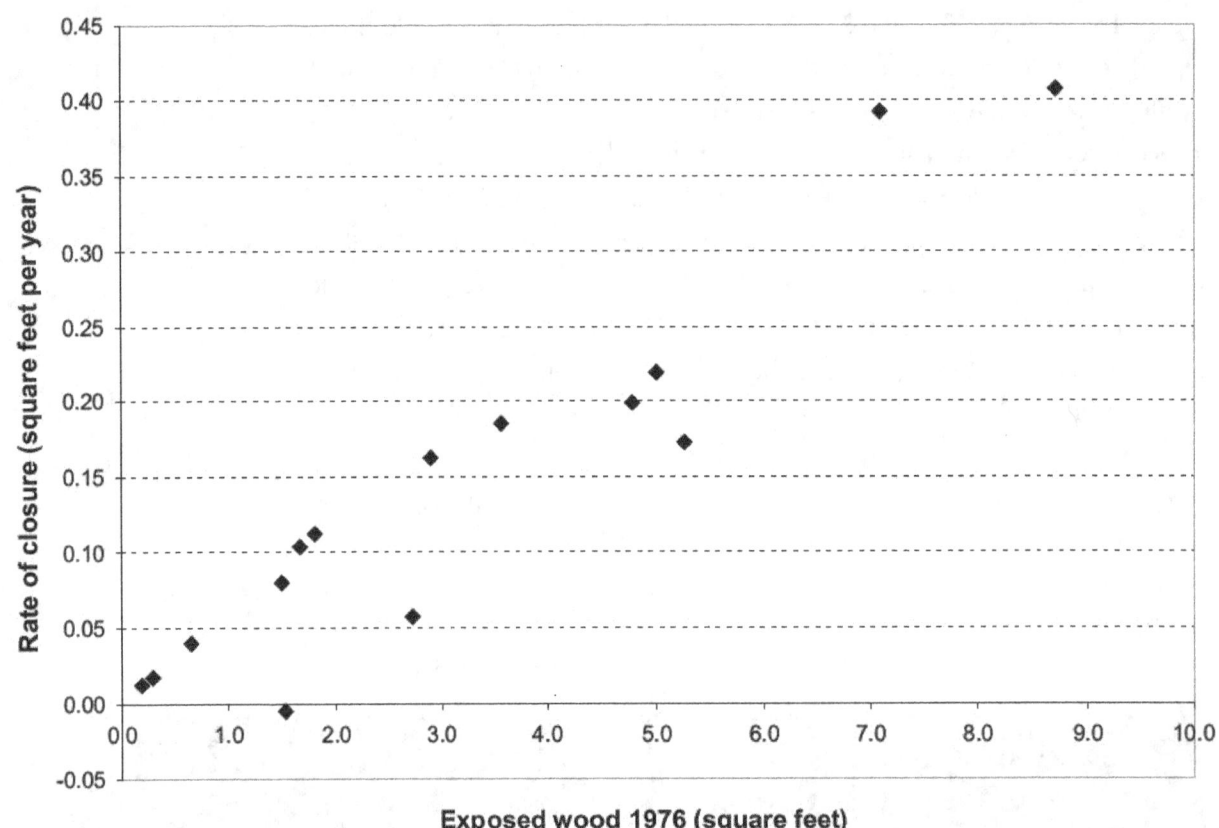

Figure 4—Mean annual rate of closure of bear-damaged bole related to area of damaged bole. Equation: $Y = 0.0033 + 0.0458X$; $r^2 = 0.91$

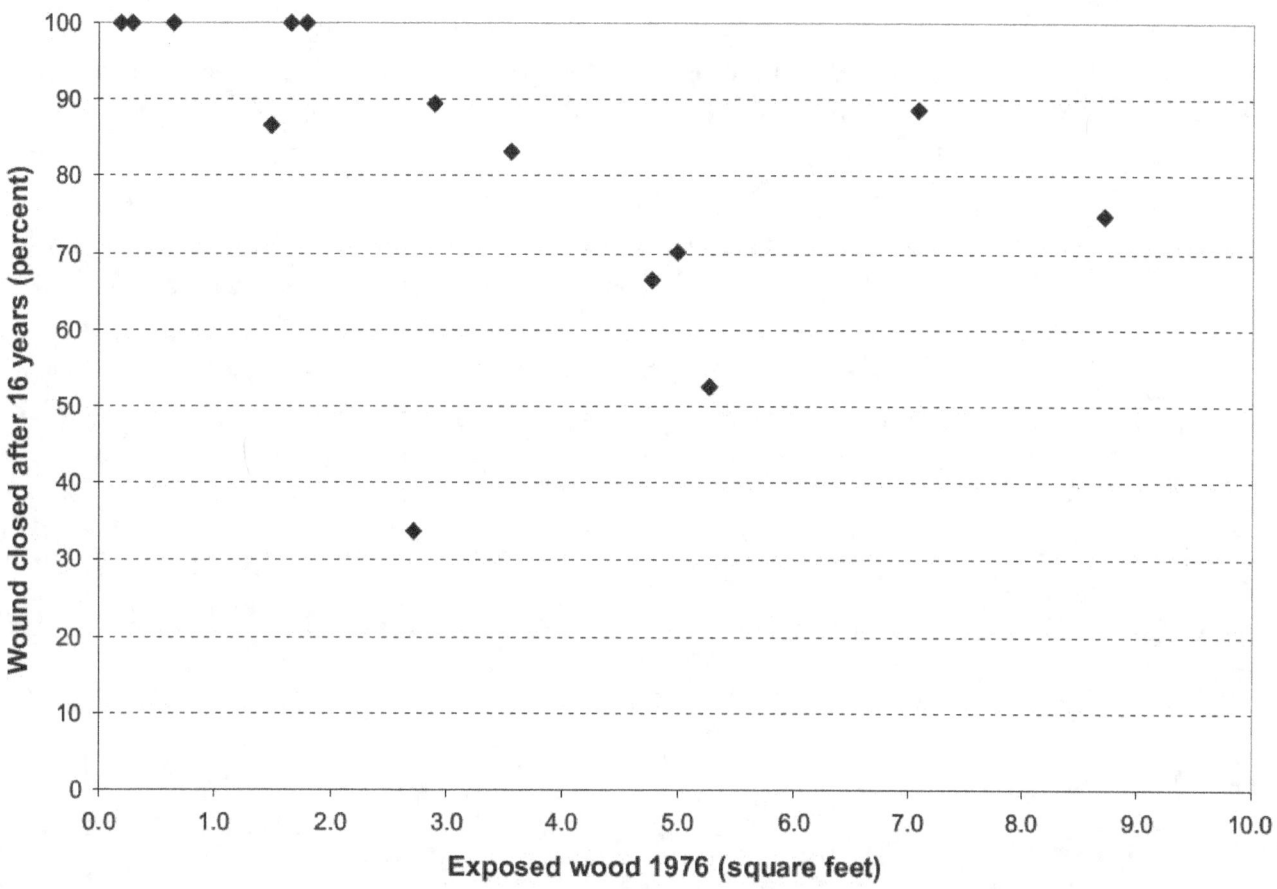

Figure 5—Percentage of wound closure related to area of bear-exposed wood.

Growth in Cross-Sectional Area of Surviving Trees

Growth at breast height—For surviving subject trees (matched and nonmatched), total 15-year growth in cross-sectional area at 4.5 ft height was related to initial d.b.h. (fig. 6). Larger trees grew faster than smaller trees, and most damaged trees of a given d.b.h. that survived the 16 years after damage grew faster than nondamaged trees. The need for log transformation was explored and rejected; stepwise regression provided the following linear equations for damaged and nondamaged trees: Y = 15-year growth (ft²): of nondamaged, Y = - 0.397 + 0.082 d.b.h.; of damaged, Y = - 0.397 + 0.097 d.b.h. The fact that the regression slopes differed for damaged and nondamaged trees (p = 0.05) precluded use of covariance analysis to calculate and statistically test adjusted means for the two groups.

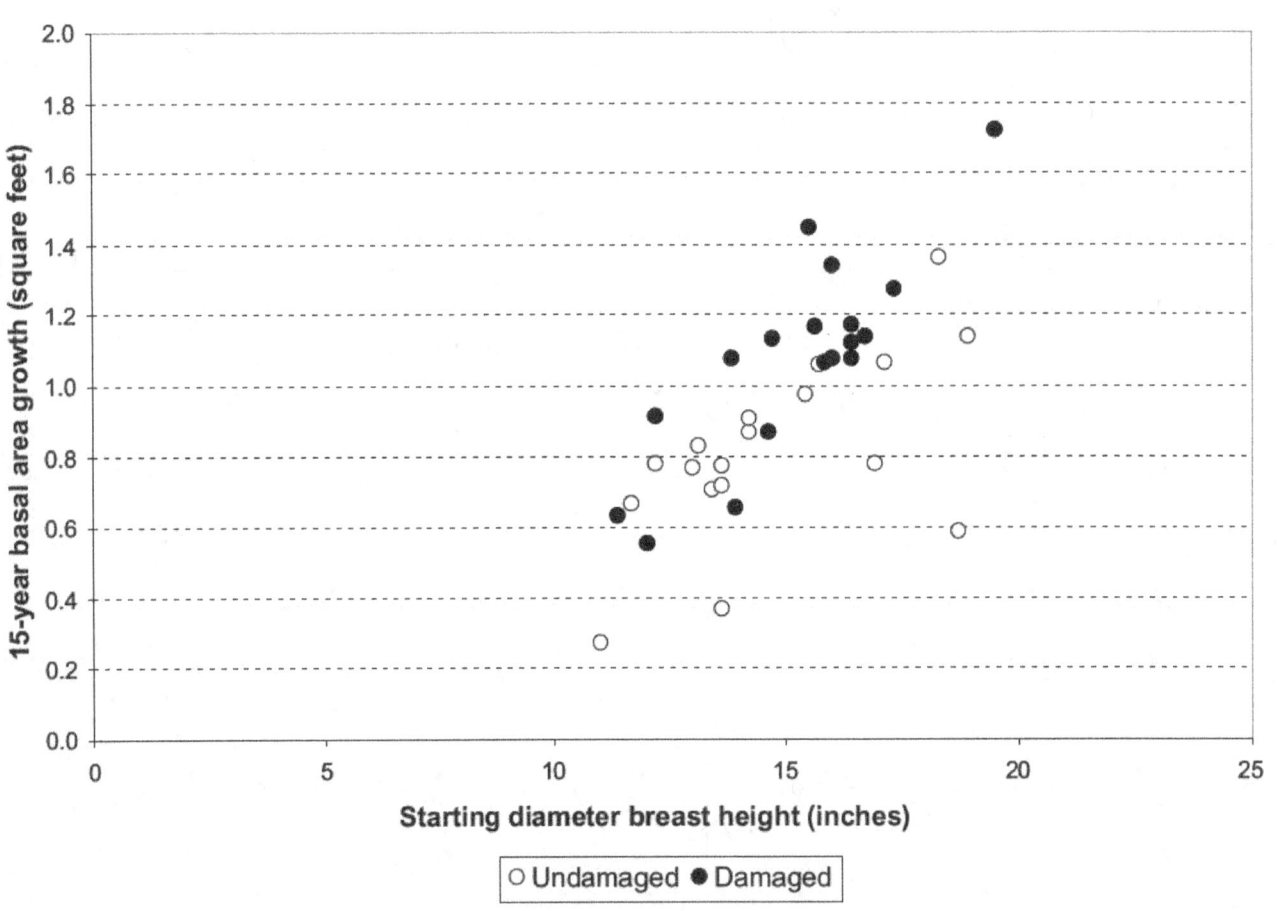

Figure 6—15-year basal area growth at breast height related to starting diameter at breast height of all surviving bear-damaged and nondamaged trees that were measured in this study.

Matched pairs—Although we initially selected 23 pairs of matched trees in 1976, one or both members of 5 pairs died between 1976 and 1991, which resulted in 18 surviving pairs for analysis of cross-sectional growth. Diameter outside bark of these 36 paired trees was measured at 6.0 ft and 4.5 ft above the mean soil surface, and above the damaged area (0.7 to 3.6 ft above mean soil level). Nondamaged trees were measured at the same three heights as their damaged counterparts. Paired t-tests compared growth in cross-sectional area (in square feet as derived from d.o.b. measurements) and starting d.o.b. of damaged and nondamaged trees (table 3). Douglas-fir that survived removal of bark from 9 to 92 percent of their basal circumference averaged 29 to 33 percent faster growth than nearby nondamaged trees of similar size. Cross-sectional growth at three levels on bear-damaged Douglas-fir was related positively to initial d.o.b. (fig. 6). Although d.o.b. of matched damaged trees averaged 3 to 6 percent larger than nondamaged (table 3), difference in mean starting d.o.b. was significant only at the level closest to the wounding (p = 0.07, table 3). Because increase in cross-sectional growth was similar at the three measurement heights, we infer no anticipated exaggeration of growth above the damaged area, hence, no measurable change in lower bole form after bear damage.

To explain this unexpected increase in growth rate after partial girdling, we initially speculated that greater losses of neighboring trees, hence greater release, could have occurred near bear-damaged trees than near nondamaged trees. To examine this possible explanation, we computed a CSI for each subject tree in 1974, 1980, 1983, and 1992 based on distance to neighboring trees (within about 40 ft) and their respective d.b.h. in these years (Arney 1973).

Initial CSI for the 18 surviving pairs of damaged trees (251 to 602 CSI units) and nondamaged trees (210 to 639) spanned a similarly wide range. Initial CSI for damaged trees averaged 382 and was only 4 CSI units more than nondamaged. The initial difference was nonsignificant (p = 0.89, table 4). Subsequently in both groups, some trees increased in CSI and others decreased. Differences in average CSI between damaged and nondamaged trees at various times before and after damage were nonsignificant (table 4). Moreover, growth at breast height was not related to the total 18-year change in CSI (fig. 7).

Damage severity and growth—Growth at breast height was related nonlinearly to damage severity (fig. 8). Average cross-sectional growth at 4.5 ft of slightly damaged trees was similar to that of nondamaged trees (0.81 ft^2 in 15 years, table 3). Periodic growth of more severely damaged trees increased to about 1.40 ft^2 where 40 to 50 percent of bole circumference was debarked, but decreased sharply to

Table 3—Means and standard errors (in parentheses) of 15-year growth and starting diameter outside bark (d.o.b.) at three heights in damaged and nondamaged trees (18 matched pairs)[a]

Height	15-year growth					Starting d.o.b.				
	Damage	Nondamaged	Difference	Percent	p-value	Damaged	Nondamaged	Difference	Percent	p-value
	- - - - - - - - - Square feet - - - - - - - - -					- - - - - - - - - - - Inches - - - - - - - - -				
6.0 feet	0.97 (0.06)	0.75 (0.06)	0.22 (0.07)	29	0.01	14.7 (0.5)	14.2 (0.5)	0.5	3.5	0.25
4.5 feet	1.08 (.07)	0.81 (.06)	.27 (.07)	33	.00	15.2 (.5)	14.7 (.4)	.5	3.4	.20
Above debarked area	1.23 (.08)	0.93 (.08)	.30 (.08)	32	.01	16.5 (.7)	15.6 (.7)	.9	5.8	.07

[a]Results from paired t-tests.

Table 4—Means, standard errors, and differences in competitive stress index (CSI) for bear-damaged and nondamaged trees near Carson, Washington (18 matched pairs)[a]

Item	Damaged		Nondamaged		Difference		
	Mean	SE	Mean	SE	CSI	Percent	p-value
	- - - - - - - - - - - - - - - - - CSI units - - - - - - - - - - - - - - - -						
Starting CSI (1974)	382	(25)	378	(22)	4	1.1	0.89
Midpoint CSI (1983)	412	(24)	429	(26)	-17	-4.0	.58
Ending CSI (1991)	385	(28)	405	(29)	-20	-4.9	.41
Net change, CSI	3	(17)	27	(17)	-24	-89	.19

[a]Results from paired t-tests.

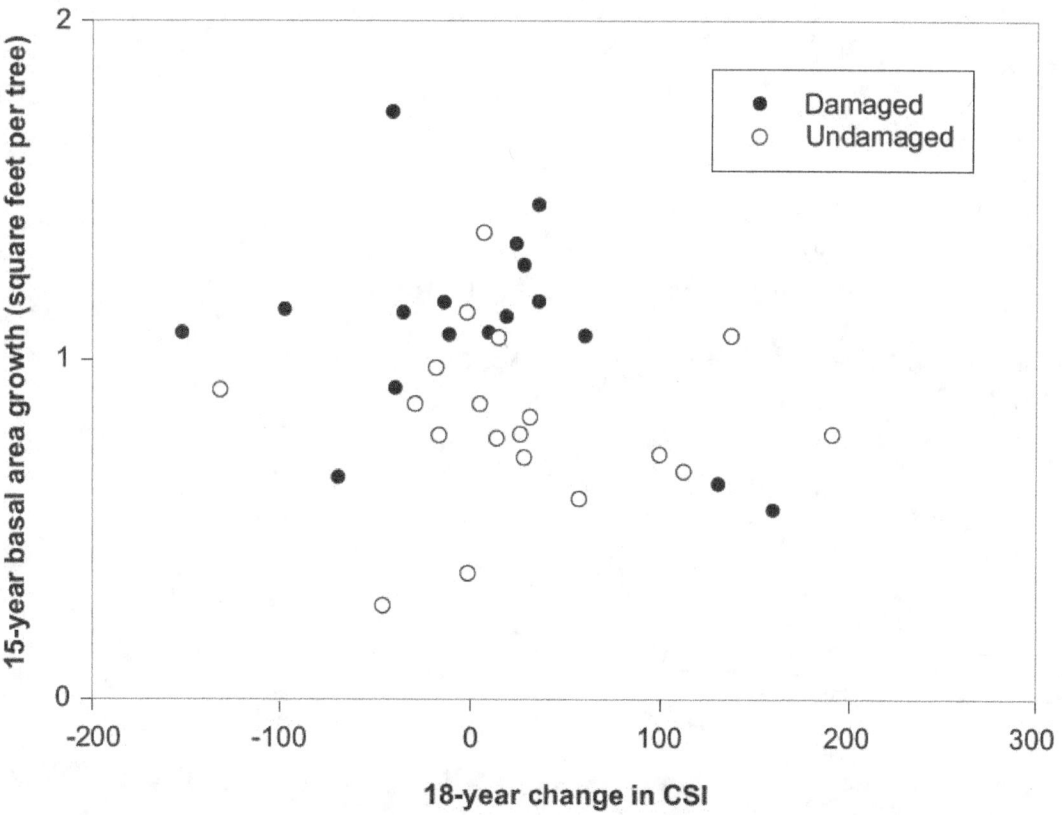

Figure 7—Fifteen-year basal area growth at breast height of bear-damaged and matched, nondamaged trees related to 18-year change in competitive stress index (CSI) (1974 to 1992).

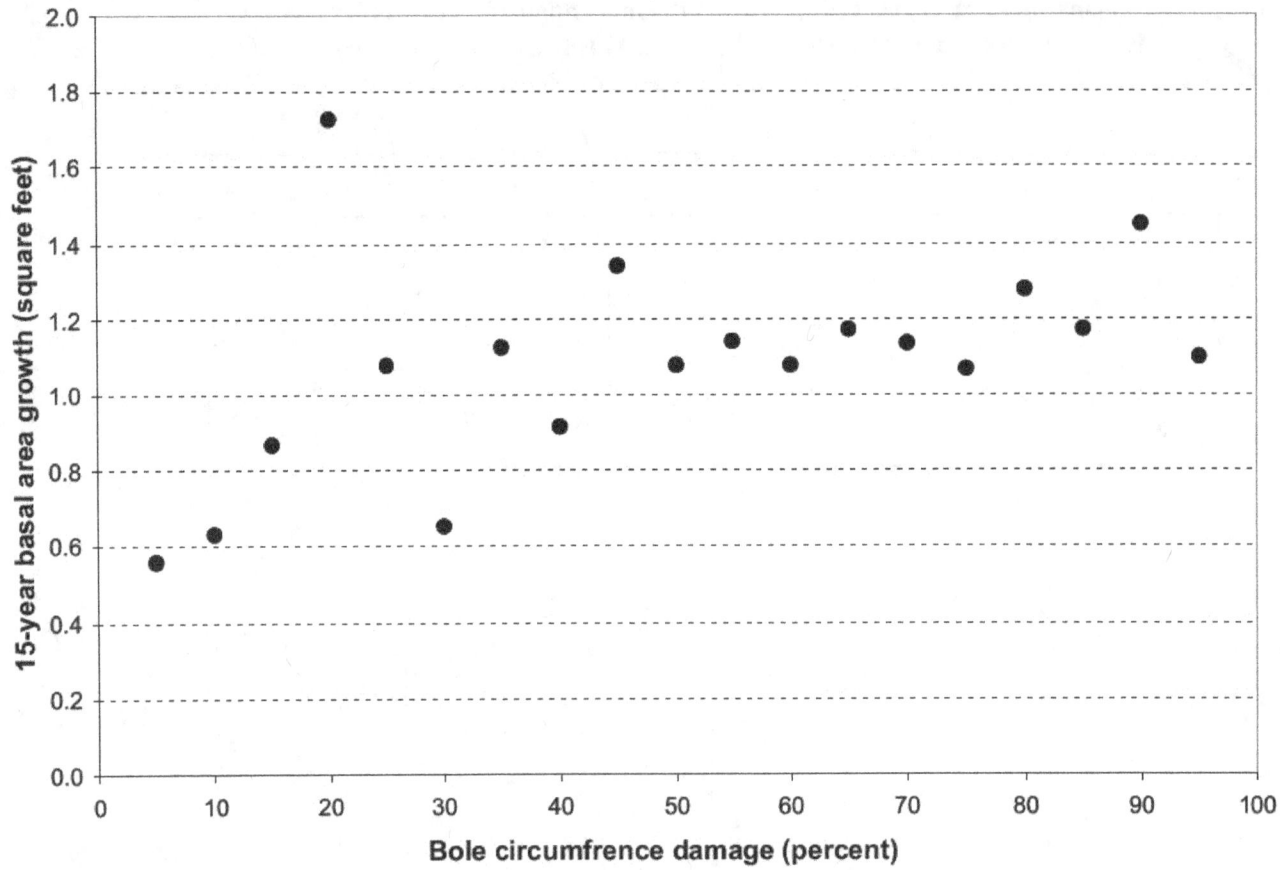

Figure 8—Fifteen-year basal area growth at breast height related to damage severity (percentage of bole circumference damaged)

zero growth or premature death in those trees with 94 to 100 percent of their basal circumference girdled (fig. 8). As expected, most severely girdled trees died sooner than those with incidental damage.

Effects on Stand Yield

In 1974 (and before bear damage), bole volume (CVTS) of live Douglas-fir in the mixed stand averaged 3,087 ft³/acre vs. 2,821 ft³/acre in the pure stand (table 5). The mean difference, 266 ft³ (9.4 percent), was not statistically significant (p = 0.27). Additional volume of live red alder in 1974 in the mixed stand averaged 2,200 ft³/acre. As a ratio of total Douglas-fir volume, merchantable volume (CV6) averaged 0.71 in the mixed stand but only 0.45 in the pure stand (table 5).

Table 5—Means and differences in live Douglas-fir volume at age 46 (1974) and age 67 years (1995) in the mixed and the pure plantation near Carson, Washington, by merchantability standard

Standard[a]	Mixed	Pure	Difference (SE)		
			------- *Cubic feet per acre* -----	*Percent*	*p-value*
			Age 46		
CVTS	3,087	2,821	266 (197)	9.4	0.27
CV6	2,205	1,275	929 (240)	72.9	.03
CV6/CVTS	0.71	0.45	-- --	--	--
			Age 67		
CVTS	5,626	5,230	396 (817)	7.6	0.66
CV6	4,973	4,018	955 (864)	23.8	.35
CV6/CVTS	0.88	0.77	-- --	--	--
			Net Change, age 46 to 67		
CVTS	2,539	2,409	130 --	5.4	--
CV6	2,768	2,743	25 --	0.9	--

[a] CVTS = cubic volume total stem, trees 1.6 in diameter at breast height (d.b.h.) and larger; CV6 = merchantable cubic volume to a 6-in top diameter, trees 7.6 in d.b.h. and larger.

Between 1974 and 1977, damage by bear, ice, and snow strongly affected stand volume and growth of both species in the mixed stand. Specifically, full or partial girdling of Douglas-fir by bear occurred early in the 1976 growing season (47 years after planting); ice and snow in winter 1976 broke tops of most red alder trees. Growth and cumulative volume of live red alder gradually declined (fig. 9A). By about 1977, total live volume of Douglas-fir (1.6-in d.b.h. and larger) in the mixed stand still exceeded that in the pure stand; however, 3 years later (1980 or five growing seasons after bear damage), total live volume was similar because of greater losses of Douglas-fir trees in the mixed stand (fig. 9A). Thereafter, net volume growth of Douglas-fir in the mixed stand recovered and exceeded that in the pure Douglas-fir stand. By 67 years after planting (1995), CVTS of Douglas-fir in the mixed stand averaged 5,626 ft³/acre, exceeding that in the pure stand by 396 ft³/acre or by 7.6 percent (table 5).

Despite an average per-acre loss of 11 large, bear-killed Douglas-fir, volume of merchantable (CV6) Douglas-fir in the mixed stand remained greater than that in the pure stand (fig. 9B). Net total increase in both CVTS and CV6 (1974-95) were similar for Douglas-fir in the mixed stand and the pure stand (table 5). Loss of large trees in the mixed stand, and in-growth into merchantable size in the pure stand are likely explanations. No attempt was made to estimate decay losses that may have been greater in bear-damaged trees.

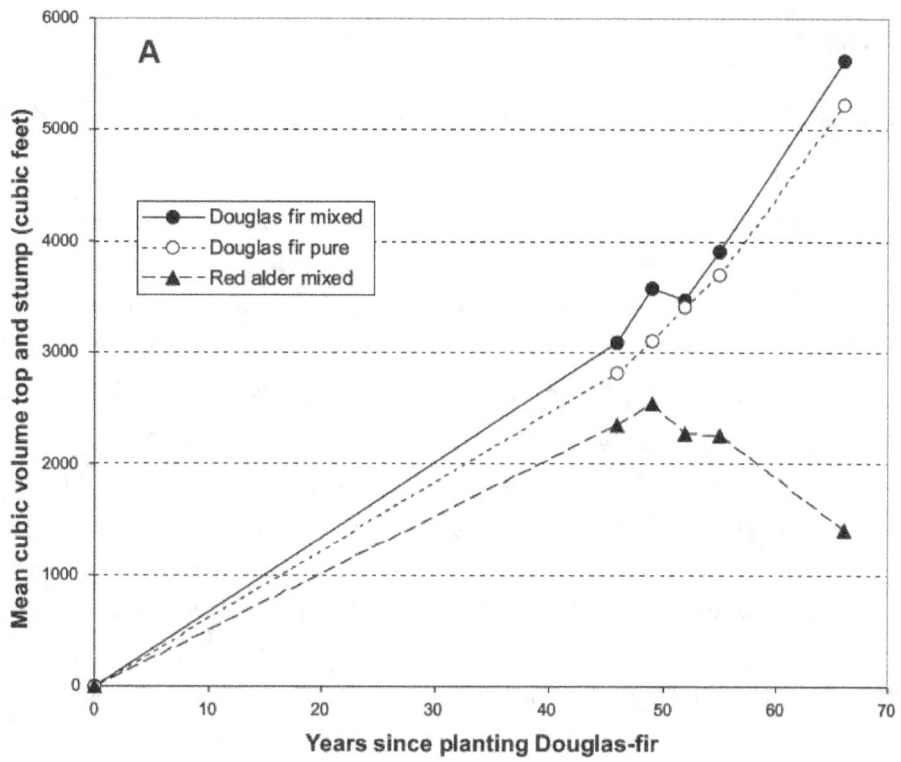

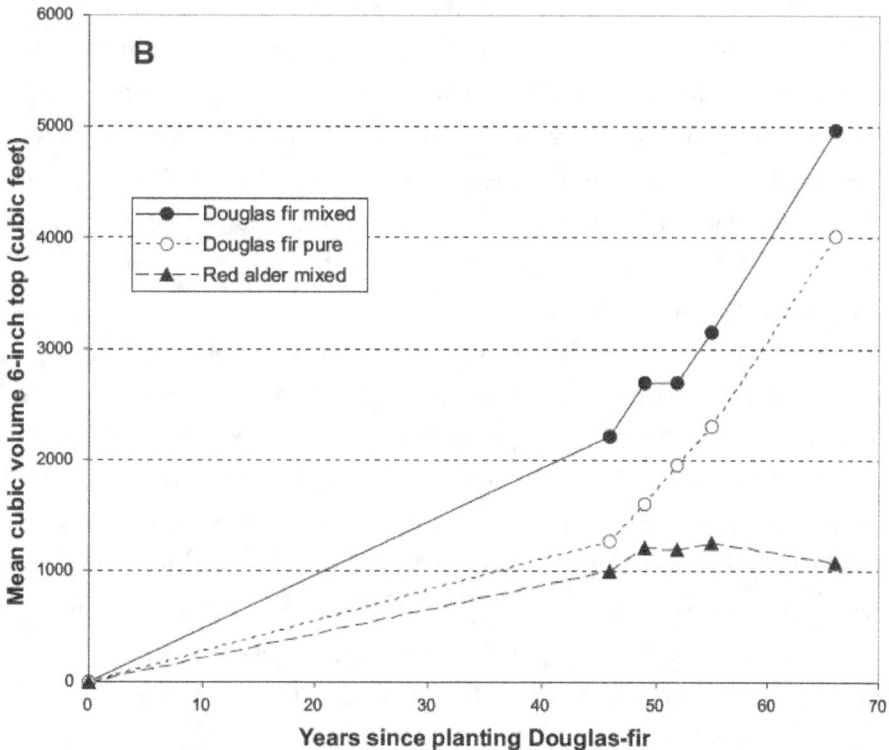

Figure 9—Trends of mean live stand volume (1974-1994) in the Douglas-fir (DF) red alder (RA) stand, by species. A total bole volume (CVTS). B. Merchantable volume to 6-in top diameter (CV6).

Discussion

Incidence and Reoccurrence of Damage

Although bear damage at our location occurred in spring as commonly reported for other locations, damage can occur over several months (Hartwell and Johnson 1988, Stewart and others 1999). For example, one small black bear girdled and killed at least 693 conifers between April 24 and July 2, 1987 in a 16-year-old, recently thinned Douglas-fir plantation (Hartwell and Johnson 1988). Of the total number of damaged trees, 48 percent had been damaged previously by bears, compared to 14 percent in our older plantation (table 1). In younger Douglas-fir–red alder stands near Olympia, Washington, 10 to 26 percent of the live Douglas-fir were damaged by bear, and most of this damage had occurred in years preceding the year of survey (table 6).

We surmise that one or more bears were attracted periodically to Douglas-fir in our mixed stand because these trees were more advanced phenologically and in amounts of new sapwood than were trees in the pure stand. For decades, Douglas-fir in the mixed stand have been visibly larger than trees in the pure stand, despite greater tree and basal area stocking in the mixed stand. The faster growth is likely explained by the nitrogen (N)-fixing capacity of associated red alder, which greatly benefits Douglas-fir at this N-deficient site (Miller and Murray 1978). Although the growth-stimulating effect of the red alder admixture at this location extends about 50 ft into the adjacent pure Douglas-fir plantation on either side (Miller and others 1993), periodic bear damage was restricted to large Douglas-fir in and within about 10 ft of the mixed stand and to Douglas-fir associated with volunteer red alder (fig.1). We speculate that much sparser understory vegetation in the mixed-species stands may facilitate bear travel and foraging.

Others have reported that both N fertilization (Kimball and others 1998b) and thinning can stimulate tree growth and increase incidence of bear damage. Nelson (1989) and Nelson and others (1994) reported that plots fertilized with urea (46 percent N) had three to four times more Douglas-fir killed by bear than nonfertilized plots at a study area near Sandy, Oregon. Fertilization with N, however, does not always enhance incidence of bear damage. Within 600 ft of our study area and in the same Douglas-fir plantation, trees responded strongly to ammonium nitrate fertilizer applied 20 years earlier, but none were damaged by bear (Miller and Tarrant 1983). A greater incidence of bear damage in thinned stands is more consistently reported (Kimball and other 1998b, Lawrence and others 1961, Maser 1967, Mason and Adams 1989, Poelker and Hartwell 1973, Schmidt and Gourley 1992). For 15 thinned and 9 nonthinned polygons in the western Cascade Range

Table 6—Summary of bear-damage surveys by specified authors

Stand		Sampled		Douglas-fir					Bark removed (percentage of circumference)			Reference
				All		Bark removed						
Age	Type[a]	Acres	Month-year	Live	Dead	Recent	1+yr	Both	0-55	56-99	100	
				Number per acre		*- - - - - - - Percent live trees - - - - - - -*			*- - - - - - - - - - -*			
16	DF	0.6	5-1987	269	33[b]	27	8	35	--	21	7	Hartwell and Johnson (1988)
30	DF/RA	2.3	9-1972	81	--	4	6	10	47	21	32	Hartwell (1973)
40	DF/RA	3.5	9-1972	58	--	4	22	26	52	18	30	Hartwell (1973)
50	DF/RA	.8	10-1976	258	--	14	2	16	39	43	18	This report

[a] DF = Douglas-fir, RA = red alder.

[b] These 33 trees per acre died in a 3-year period after precommercial thinning; of these trees, 24 per acre died from bear damage and 19 more per acre (7 percent) were likely to die in the next year. This totaled 43 bear-killed trees per acre or 14 percent of the original 302 trees per acre.

of Oregon examined in 1989, Kanaskie and others (1990) reported that 93 percent of the thinned and 44 percent of the nonthinned polygon stands were damaged by bear in spring 1988. Yet, a corresponding survey with about 60 polygons in each group in coastal Oregon stands showed no difference in incidence of bear damage between thinned and nonthinned polygons.

Discrepancies exist in the literature about what tissue of conifers is eaten by black bears. Our observations agree with those of Poelker and Hartwell (1973) and Radwan (1969). After removing bark, bears used their canine teeth to remove new sapwood, which has a relatively high concentration of simple sugars (Radwan 1969). The one-cell-thick cambium, which separates the inner bark (phloem) and the new sapwood, probably was also consumed. Although we saw no evidence that inner bark was consumed as reported by Schmidt and Gourley (1992: 309, 312), Larry Irvin in Idaho has seen inner bark scraped by bears after the bark was stripped from conifer trees.[4]

Severity and Consequences of Damage

Damage severity in 1976, expressed as percentage of bole circumference with bared sapwood, ranged between 9 and 100 percent on the 28 trees in the four 0.2-acre plots (equivalent to 35 damaged trees per acre). Frequencies of specified damage severity classes differ greatly among locations reported by Hartwell and Johnson (1988) and Hartwell (1973) for younger stands near Olympia, Washington (table 6).

Foliage color or loss is the current basis for aerial detection of bear damage (Kanaskie and others 1990). Trees with red, brown, or yellow foliage are visually detectable. Completely girdled trees show color changes in foliage, but partially girdled trees seldom do. After complete girdling at our study site, foliage color regressed from dark green to red-brown in a 2- to 14-year period. Others report that this regression to red-brown color and even needle loss occurs within 1 year of complete girdling (Hartwell and Johnson 1988). Kanaskie and others (1990: 20) quoted forestry consultant Bob Gilman's observation that "girdled trees on hotter, drier sites change color more rapidly than girdled trees on more favorable sites." Although our north-facing study area probably has favorable microclimate, a probable additional reason for the slower rate of color change and tree death in our study area is root grafting between damaged and nondamaged trees. This speculation is based on calloused-over stumps that we observed on a portion of the stand that had been precommercially thinned about 25 years earlier. Although complete girdling by bear may have stopped downward movement of photosynthate from the crowns

---

[4] Irwin, Larry L. 2003. Personal communication. Principal scientist, National Council for Air and Stream Improvement, Inc., P.O. Box 68, Stevensville, MT 59870.

of girdled trees, root systems of damaged trees probably survived by receiving photosynthate from one or more nearby trees. Thereby enhanced, roots and sapwood of damaged trees could continue to deliver water and nutrients to crowns of damaged trees.

Our completely girdled trees died within 14 years. The survivors were partially girdled trees (bark removed from 9 to 92 percent of circumference). Of these trees, 83 percent (19 of 23) survived the 16-year period of observation. Although small areas of debarking completely closed within 16 growing seasons, larger areas remained exposed despite gradual encroachment of bark.

Our statistical analysis that related duration of tree survival to severity of bole damage serves to demonstrate a potentially useful technique to predict years to death after varying severities of debarking. Our analysis was limited because (1) only one site was sampled, (2) only a small number of trees were available, and (3) no data were recorded in the interval between 5 and 12 years. Moreover, year-to-death was not known accurately for the completely girdled tree recorded as dead at year 14.

In our comparison of 18 surviving d.b.h.-matched pairs, partially girdled trees averaged about 30 percent faster growth in cross-sectional area at 6.0 and 4.5 ft height, and immediately above the area of debarking. We attempted to eliminate potential explanations for this surprising finding. Difference in initial size of damaged vs. nondamaged trees was not an explanation. Moreover, differences in starting or ending CSI were similar for both groups. Finally, growth at b.h. was unrelated to change in CSI. We remain perplexed as to the cause of enhanced growth after partial girdling by bear.

Bear damage temporarily reduced stand growth and potential yield by killing some large trees (about 11 per acre). Although few in number, these were among the largest trees in the stand. Consequently, net gains in total live-tree volume (and potential yield per acre) were reduced for several years, until growth of the remaining trees compensated for the volume lost to mortality. Surprisingly, accelerated growth of partially girdled trees contributed to the rapid recovery of volume yield in this mixed stand after bear damage.

Results at our study area do not erase a current concern among foresters and landowners that yield could be reduced by bear damage. We infer from the literature, however, that the magnitude of yield and income losses after the bear damage will differ greatly among individual stands for the following reasons:

• Bear damage is a sporadic event of varying severity as to numbers of trees damaged and percentage of debarked bole.

- Bears select fast-growing trees with above-average diameter. Completely girdled trees eventually die, but death can occur within 6 months to 14 years after damage. Depending on their size and numbers, some bear-killed trees can be salvaged in some situations. Wood decay may reduce amount of recoverable volume. Otherwise, live stand volume and volume growth are reduced until growth of remaining trees compensate for that lost by mortality. We anticipate that the effects of bear-killed trees on yield could be similar to those of thinning-from-above; growth of subordinate, especially shade-tolerant species is likely to be enhanced by loss of dominant Douglas-fir.
- Rotation length will have an important effect. The shorter the rotation, the less time to compensate for damage.
- Partially girdled Douglas-fir trees can actually grow faster in diameter. The extent to which this surprising consequence may occur at other locations is unknown. Confirmation could be derived readily by comparing growth of bear-damaged trees on existing research plots at numerous locations that span the range of environmental conditions in the Douglas-fir type.

Conclusions

- Black bears damaged coast Douglas-fir trees in this stand on at least four occasions between 1929 (planting) and 1991; damage was most extensive in 1976 when 35 trees per acre were damaged.
- Most completely girdled trees died within 5 years of damage; one tree died by 14 years. Tree death was probably delayed at this location because root systems of bear-damaged and nondamaged trees were linked.
- Partial girdling (40 to 50 percent of circumference) enhanced growth in cross-sectional area above the highest damaged area, and by a similar 30 percent at 4.5 and 6.0 ft above the mean soil surface. No change in bole form occurred.
- As a result of bears killing about 11 large Douglas-fir trees per acre, live stand volume of this species was reduced for several years until growth of the remaining damaged and nondamaged trees compensated for the volume lost to mortality.

Acknowledgments

The authors thank Dean DeBell for alerting us to the incidence of bear damage in 1976 so we could measure and document its consequences in a timely manner. We thank James Arney for providing a computer program to estimate CSI, Brian Biswell for testing and using this program, and Tim Harrington for guiding our multiple-regression analyses. Technical reviews of our draft manuscript were provided by Steve Caffareta, Pat Cunningham, Mark Gourley, Larry Irwin, and Doug Robin.

Metric Equivalents

When you know:	Multiply by:	To find:
Inches (in)	2.54	Centimeters
Feet (ft)	.305	Meters
Acres (ac)	.405	Hectares
Trees per acre (TPA)	2.47	Trees per hectare
Cubic feet per acre (ft³/acre)	.07	Cubic meters per hectare
Pounds per acre (lb/acre)	1.12	kilograms per hectare

Literature Cited

Allison, P.D. 1995. Survival analysis using the SAS system: a practical guide. SAS Institute, Inc. Cary, NC. 292 p.

Arney, J.D. 1973. Tables for quantifying competitive stress on individual trees. Info. Rep. BC-X-78. Victoria, BC: Canadian Forest Service. 10 p.

Brackett, M. 1973. Notes on tariff tree volume computation. Resour. Manage. Rep. 24. Olympia, WA: Washington State Department of Natural Resources. 26 p.

Bruce, D.; DeMars, D.J. 1974. Volume equations for second-growth Douglas-fir. Res. Note PNW-239. Portland, OR: U.S. Department of Agriculture, Forest Service, Pacific Northwest Forest and Range Experiment Station. 5 p.

Childs, T.; Worthington, N. 1955. Bear damage to young Douglas-fir. Res. Note PNW-RN-113. Portland, OR: U.S. Department of Agriculture, Forest Service, Pacific Northwest Forest and Range Experiment Station. 4 p.

Hartwell, H.D. 1973. A survey of tree debarking by black bear in Capitol Forest. DNR Notes 7. Olympia, WA: Department of Natural Resources. 7 p.

Hartwell, H.D.; Johnson, L.E. 1988. Silvicultural effects of basal girdling by black bear in a young Douglas-fir plantation. Olympia, WA: Washington State Department of Natural Resources. 28 p.

Hosmer, D.W., Jr.; Lemeshow, S. 1999. Applied survival analysis: regression modeling of time to event data. New York: John Wiley and Sons, Inc. 386 p.

Kanaskie, A.; Chetock, J.; Irwin, G.; Overhulser, D. 1990. Black bear damage to forest trees in northwest Oregon. Pest Manage. Rep. 90-1. Salem, OR: Oregon Department of Forestry. 34 p.

Kimball, B.A.; Nolte D.L.; Engeman, R.M.; Johnston, J.J.; Stermitz, F.R. 1998a. Chemically mediated foraging preference of black bear (*Ursus americanus*). Journal of Mammalogy. 79: 448-456.

Kimball, B.A.; Turnblom, E.C.; Nolte, D.L.; Griffin, D.L.; Engeman, R.M. 1998b. Effects of thinning and nitrogen fertilization on sugars and terpenes in Douglas-fir vascular tissues: implications for black bear foraging. Forest Science. 44(4): 599-602.

King, J.E. 1968. Site index curves for Douglas-fir in the Pacific Northwest. Weyerhaeuser For. Pap. 8. Centralia, WA: Weyerhaeuser Co. 49 p. + illustrations.

Maser, C. 1967. Black bear damage to Douglas-fir in Oregon. The Murrelet. 48: 34-38.

Mason, A.C.; Adams, D.L. 1989. Black bear damage to thinned timber stands in northwest Montana. Western Journal of Applied Forestry. 4: 10-13.

Miller, R.E.; Murray, M.D. 1978. The effects of red alder on growth of Douglas-fir. In: Briggs, D.G.; DeBell, D.S.; Atkinson, W.A., comps. Utilization and management of alder. Gen. Tech. Rep. PNW-GTR-70. Portland, OR: U.S. Department of Agriculture, Forest Service, Pacific Northwest Forest and Range Experiment Station: 283-306.

Miller, R.E.; Reukema, D.L.; Max, T.A. 1993. Size of Douglas-fir trees in relation to distance from a mixed red-alder–Douglas-fir stand. Canadian Journal of Forest Research. 23: 1413-1418.

Miller, R.E.; Tarrant, R.F. 1983. Long-term growth response of Douglas-fir to ammonium nitrate fertilizer. Forest Science. 29: 127-137.

Nelson, E.E. 1989. Black bears prefer urea-fertilized trees. Western Journal of Applied Forestry. 4: 13-15.

Nelson, E.E.; McWilliams, M.G.; Thies, W.G. 1994. Mortality and growth of urea-fertilized Douglas-fir on a *Phellinus weirii*-infested site in Oregon. Western Journal of Applied Forestry. 9(2): 52-56.

Neter, J.; Wasserman, W.; Kutner, M.H. 1989. Applied linear regression models. 2nd ed., Homewood, IL: Irwin Press. 667 p.

Poelker, R.J.; Hartwell, H.D. 1973. Black bear of Washington. Biol. Bull. 14. Olympia, WA: Washington State Game Department. 180 p. + illustrations.

Radwan, M.A. 1969. Chemical composition of the sapwood of four tree species in relation to feeding by the black bear. Forest Science. 15: 11-16.

SAS Institute Inc. 1988. SAS/STAT user's guide, version 6.03 ed. Cary, NC: SAS Institute Inc.

Schmidt, W.C.; Gourley, M. 1992. Black bear. In: Black, H.C., tech. ed. Silvicultural approaches to animal damage management in Pacific Northwest forests. Gen. Tech. Rep. PNW-GTR-287. Portland, OR: U.S. Department of Agriculture, Forest Service, Pacific Northwest Research Station: 309-331.

Shea, K.R. 1967. Effect of artificial root and bole injuries on diameter increment of Douglas-fir. Weyerhaeuser For. Pap. 11. Centralia, WA: Weyerhaeuser Company. 11 p.

Stewart, W.B.; Witmer, G.W.; Koehler, G.M. 1999. Black bear damage to forest stands in western Washington. Western Journal of Applied Forestry. 14: 128-131.

Sullivan, T.P. 1993. Feeding damage by bears in managed forests of western hemlock-western red cedar in midcoastal British Columbia. Canadian Journal of Forest Research. 23: 49-54.

Tarrant, R.F.; Miller, R.E. 1963. Accumulation of organic matter and soil nitrogen beneath a plantation of red alder and Douglas-fir. Soil Science Society of America Proceedings. 27: 231-234.